Banners in His Name

A second book on banners for the Church of Christ

Edited and compiled by
PRISCILLA NUNNERLEY

This book is dedicated to all those who have contributed.

By the same author:
An Army with Banners
First published 1982
Reprinted 1984

© *Priscilla Nunnerley 1985*
First published in 1986

ISBN 0 9509307 1 7

Designed and printed in England by
Nuprint Services Limited, Harpenden, Herts AL5 4SE

Contents

*We are very grateful for
the kind permission of
different churches to print
photographs and drawings.*

Introduction

It has been a joy to edit this book including contributions from so many people. In January 1985 we (The King's Church, Amersham, formerly Amersham Christian Fellowship) hosted a 'Banner Day' at the Baptist Chapel and some of the chapters and photographs are a result of this event. Thank you so very much to everyone who has contributed.

This is the sequel to 'An Army with Banners' which is a handbook for those starting banner-making. It was written and printed privately in 1982, in faith, and to our delight has sold 3,000 copies. The second book is written to share what is happening now and to give many practical ideas.

Banner-making essentially involves a group of people waiting on the Lord for His direction. This removes the emphasis from the skills and efforts of the people involved, focusing it on God's inspiration and guidance through the gift of His Holy Spirit.

After a year away from making banners I returned with a conviction that simplicity is the key. Simplicity can include beautiful fabric, colour, and tassels but it says one thing. It communicates directly and effectively.

Our present group comprises four people and we are meeting on Monday evenings this autumn. Anne had the idea for the present project and we have together worked it out. It is taking us much longer than we anticipated and we have a delightful sense of unhurriedness and plenty of fun and chat. I do feel that if possible banner-making should be a relaxation.

As well as more weighty themes we sometimes do ones with a light touch with balloons or flowers etc. They are done quickly and can have casual letters.

The process of sewing in itself can be an offering. A nun once wrote 'Through the eye of your needle sew a kiss of heaven'. Lest the mention of sewing should deter the men let it be said that banner-making is equally for them! Don't forget Bezalel and Oholiab! We invite people to join us for a session which is usually eight weeks, a shortened version of the school term. Some may stay for several years, others less because they have family commitments or move on to other activities in the church. Other groups may have very different arrangements. We find that five people are the largest workable number.

We will probably not have time this Christmas to make anything new but will use one made several years ago. We feel we should not make banners just for the sake of it and when the Lord told us to stop we stopped for almost a year. Banner-making is not an indispensable priority.

It may be that you will make just one, or perhaps in reading this book you will decide that banner-making is not for you but you will feel encouraged in another creative gift.

Banners are for sharing. Recently we have made three in Spanish for friends in Peru to use in street meetings. Some of our young people used others with street drama and evangelism. The conclusion at the Banner Day was that we should take banners out using them in different ways to communicate the gospel. The chapter 'Outreach' is a result of this discussion.

Although it is good to have fresh inspiration for each banner it is impossible to be entirely original and so you are welcome to use some of these ideas and designs in creating your own.

> 'Prepare the way for the people.
> Build up, build up the highway!
> Remove the stones.
> Raise a banner for the nations'.
>
> Isaiah 62:10

Simplicity is the key to this banner in the chapel at Amersham.

The Name of Jesus

by Neil Bartlett

My wife and I were both teachers and when faced with the problem of choosing a name for our child we had a particular difficulty. Many names conjured up instant pictures and personalities of those in school and there were some names that stood out more than others!

When we consider the Name of Jesus we also have certain impressions of this person. However, the Name of Jesus is more important than mere impressions and we should not be surprised when it is attacked as Satan has constantly endeavoured to devalue His Name. The battle lines were drawn right from the start when seventy disciples who had been sent out by the Lord reported back, saying, 'Even the demons submit to us in your Name.'

Later, the Sanhedrin commanded Peter and John not to speak or teach in the Name of Jesus. Why did this happen? Because there is power in the Name of Jesus Christ. This power was dramatically demonstrated when Peter told the cripple at the temple gate called Beautiful, to walk in the Name of Jesus Christ of Nazareth and he walked.

As the Body of Christ we need to understand and come to terms with the fact that there is authority in the Name of Jesus. This name cannot be used as a formula tagged on the end of our prayers hoping for the same result that Aladdin had with 'open sesame'.

You and I must KNOW the authority of His Name as a reality. Jesus said, 'I will do whatever you ask in My Name, so that the Son may bring glory to the Father.' We have been given the 'power of attorney' when we use His Name. To have P.o.A. entitles one to act legally on another's behalf and when we use His Name it is just as though He does it Himself. This is only for Christians whose lives are under the authority of God's Word. It is time for us to *use* the Name of Jesus with increasing boldness as we know the TRUTH of the authority of that Name.

His Name on Banners

Perhaps the greatest privilege of the banner-maker is to raise the Name of Jesus. A key word in the scripture verses that refer to banners is 'raise' or 'raise-up'. The command is to hold aloft a standard that is a rallying point for the people. Roman triumphal processions were headed by a standard that was the focal point of their victory celebrations. As we lift up the Name of Jesus on a banner we proclaim that He is Victor, Saviour and Lord. Seeing His Name visually helps to focus our attention of Him and our spirits rejoice. We should lift up this Name far more and have more banners in future which include His Name or quote His words so that our lives may centre on Him and make Him known.

St Luke's, Watford

A Celebration Banner

Commission

To design a banner for a 3,150 cm long marquee wall for a weekend of celebrating the faith.

Plan

Worked out with prayer between three of us on two afternoons. Our aim was to be very bold, colourful and attractive and to communicate that Jesus is alive today.

The name of Jesus

Measured 122 cm × 488 cm and was made on hardboard backed with a wooden framework. Matt white emulsion paint was used for the background and the letters were gold with a touch of colour to highlight them.

The rainbow fabrics

Four metres each of the seven rainbow colours were bought in cotton poplin. A diagonal cut was made across each piece so there would be a narrower and a wider end. The pieces were joined and the ends pleated and pinned to the boards.

The side panels

Each was made of three 90 cm × 244 cm pieces of hardboard. Large paper stencil letters were drawn around on the hardboard. The letters were white with an orange background on the left and blue on the right.

A celebration banner.

JESUS

centre

I am the light of the world

left side

I am the way the truth and the life

right side

the three sections join together.

11

Why Banners?

Jesus Himself used parables to tell many things. He was a Master of visual communication; He used vivid word pictures and taught truths from the scenes around Him.

The word banner is biblical. It is used eighteen times in the Old Testament and it means victory.

There is a need in our worship and communication for a non-permanent art-form made from inexpensive materials and banner-making provides this versatility.

Banner making can be enjoyed by people of all ages and backgrounds. Today the Holy Spirit is giving creative gifts to the whole church as He did to Bezalel and his friends long ago for the building of the tabernacle.

For many, music will have deep significance; but there are those of us on whom visual art has a profound effect. Visual symbolism offers a window through which beauty and the truth of God's Word can touch our spirits. As we meditate on the words or design we are drawn beyond ourselves to focus on God.

Banners essentially speak to the spirit through the eyes. They must arrest attention and draw people to stop and look. Symbols and colours communicate to the senses and through the senses to the spirit. Therefore it is important that they are not just someone's 'good idea' but that they come through revelation from the Holy Spirit. They are a means by which God can speak and not the artist.

It is a rich experience for a group of people to create something together and offer it to God, knowing that their gift to Him may be used to influence and enrich others.

St Giles and St Andrew's, Stoke Poges, Slough.

abide in my

one another

make

walk in **LOVE** is kind

your

no fear in aim never ends

Meditation

by J. Stuart Reid

We may present our banners to the Lord as part of our worship as 'something beautiful' for God, but also our banners must be forms of communicating truth. The beauty and technical excellence of a banner is that people's attention should be caught in order that they may see the truth it is seeking to convey. They should be clearly directed by the design to see the words or the message the banner is expressing.

People should be encouraged to meditate on the Word presented before them. Meditation on God's Word leads to prosperity and success in all we do (see Joshua 1:8 and Psalm 1:2–3). To meditate means to muse on, chew over, say aloud (not too loud if it's a place of public worship!) again and again the Word of God. By meditating on the Word, we start to see how this truth will work out in our life. God's Word has got to get into our spirits before it does us good – like food which will do us no good unless we swallow it.

Pray that when people see your banner they will not stop at the skill of your handiwork or your inventive design or beautiful material, but that these will be aids to catch their attention, to lead their eye and eventually their heart to the truth you are seeking to display.

When you see a banner in a place of worship:

- Ask God the Holy Spirit to speak to you through the banner before you.
- Seek to find out what is the main message of the banner; if it is a text it is obvious.
- Speak the truth or word quietly under your breath and keep repeating and thinking about it. Someone said the Word of God is like dehydrated food, it

needs the Holy Spirit to swell it out, to enable us to enjoy it fully.

- Start pondering over the words, squeezing out all the richness of the truth in them. Keep chewing it over like food until you are able to digest the nutritional constituents into your spirit.
- Ask, 'How does this apply to my life?' and muse on it until God's Spirit speaks to you through it.
- See yourself in your imagination enjoying the good of that truth.
- Desire what you have pictured, with all your heart, keep reminding yourself of it daily from your Bible or from your memory.
- Ask the Holy Spirit to confirm this vision in your heart – until you are sure that in your spirit you have received it, according to Mark 11:24.

Then you can wait in thankfulness, until you see its outworking in your life.

Hebrews 12 1+2

The Idea or Vision

Direction

The Lord delighted to specify exact details for the furnishing of the Tabernacle even to the hem of a priestly robe having a border of gold bells and pomegranates. Should we not expect Him to direct us today?

Joy

Proverbs 8:30 speaks of Jesus with His Father at creation as 'the craftsman at His side filled with delight day after day, rejoicing always in His presence'. As we create in His company so we will experience His joy.

Inspiration

This comes in a variety of ways, as a vision that comes in a moment, as a concept that grows, as an idea that comes out of the meditation of the group as they meet together around the Word of God. It has often been our experience that, starting with an idea for the words or design, we have received inspiration step-by-step and slowly the banner has grown to completion with different people making and suggesting different parts.

    We do sense a real gift of the Holy Spirit's guidance and creativity as we work. Inspiration comes from walking with the Lord day by day, from listening to Him and through soaking a possible future project in prayer. Ideas can come during a time of worship. There is a group who spend three sessions in Bible study before they spend seven sessions making a set of banners!

Now

We seek the Lord for the word that is for now, words from the Word of God that echo deep in our hearts as relevant to the present needs of the people. The pastor or another member of the church may give us these words or we may have them ourselves. No other words have the power of the Word of God.

Struggle

There is sometimes a struggle in working out the original idea. This is often a natural part of creativity but just occasionally there may be a conflict, not with materials, scissors and needles but with principalities and powers of darkness. At such times we can declare the Name of Jesus, our position in Him and His victory over the situation. We can also stop and pray through the details of the project.

'Jesus is Lord'. The design for a large banner made of materials that were glued on. The sky is black, the figures different colours and the crown white and gold. *Christchurch Stone, Staffs.*

Banners and Prophecy

by Gill Douglas

(see back cover photograph)

We can only give to the world as much as we have amongst ourselves. As we share our lives within our groups in love and commitment so, like the alabaster box of ointment broken open so that the perfume could flow, we too are broken and God's fragrance is set free in our churches and in the world. The quality of our banners is a direct reflection of where we are with God and with each other. We can have lovely designs and beautiful craftsmanship, but the resulting banners can be empty unless we have the right foundations. Our willingness to allow God to work in our relationships allows His Spirit to flow. As we draw close to Him and to each other so He is able to speak to us and anoint our gifts.

Many of us have been given pictures from the Lord at one time or another. These are very precious, but what I long for is something more, a real 'gut' prophecy where we feel with The Lord what He feels, when we laugh with Him, and when we weep with Him, when we seek from Him the Word for our church for now.

Many of our banners, of course, come out of where we have been, but I long to see in them an expression of where we are going in our fellowships. As we waited on the Lord for our last banner the imagery of a broken world and God's people binding it together came to mind.

A few years ago I was very moved by a tape of David Pawson, expounding Habbakuk. He talked about how he longed that our expressions of worship be 'Shigionoth' (Habbakuk 4). It is a lovely word that I cannot explain but it is an expression of who God is, of His might and majesty and what His heart is saying, 'Shigionoth' translated into our songs, dance, banners etc. causes us to bow down in awe and reverence, to worship the Creator and not the creation. Catching some of David Pawson's vision and seeking the Lord for the last banner brought tears. Several weeks later when the design was almost complete – a gold lurex cross on a dark blue background, over which was superimposed a broken world with gold rays – it was suddenly clear what else was needed – an encircling ring of God's rainbow people, and the words 'Lord have mercy'.

The Symbol of the Dove

the dove resting or holding olive branch signifies peace

the ascending or descending dove symbolises the Holy Spirit

Step by Step

by Liz Waite

(see front cover photograph)

I would like to share with you a little of how our group approaches banner-making at the Church of the Holy Spirit, Bedgrove, Aylesbury.

The first step is to put the whole project before the Lord in prayer. We ask for guidance on the picture, the wording, the colours, the materials and even the sewing. Prayer has proved to be the most important part of the whole process. We have learned to come before the Lord expecting Him to answer us and give us words and pictures. I remember in the beginning thinking this only happened to very 'spiritual' people. Well, now I know that the Lord will speak to every one of us if we will wait, listen and expect to hear.

The group (three people) has developed a oneness and when making decisions we are usually unanimous. We do, however, feel at ease with each other to say 'no' if we disagree on any point and this can sometimes be very important.

When we have all agreed on a rough sketch we have it approved by Roger (our vicar) and then we go on to scale it up to represent the finished article. This is where Jan shines. She is our 'letter lady' and she designs, scales up and places the words. Once we have a full-sized copy we can go on to decide colours and materials.

Shopping for the materials has always been quite eventful and we have had many amusing moments. We have often been confronted by assistants shaking their heads and saying 'No, I'm sorry we don't have it', or 'I'm sure there won't be enough', only to find seconds later the exact requirements tucked away on a bottom shelf or in a back room.

We have also been given so many new experiences when sewing. None of us had any special training to work with materials. Each time we start a banner we seem to discover new things. Jan, who says she cannot sew at all, proved to be the only one who could embroider the snowdrops satisfactorily on our Christmas Frontal, 'Emmanuel'.

Each week we meet for an evening to plan and sew the banners although Margaret also spends time on her own doing most of the embroidery. We have had many hours of good fellowship together and have benefitted greatly from our times of prayer. In each new project we really do have a sense of the Lord leading us, step by step, as we work for Him, according to His will.

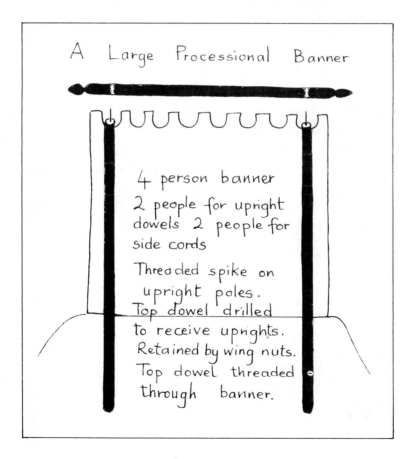

A Large Processional Banner

4 person banner
2 people for upright dowels 2 people for side cords

Threaded spike on upright poles.
Top dowel drilled to receive uprights.
Retained by wing nuts.
Top dowel threaded through banner.

You are like Salt

by Alison Eames

(see colour photograph)

The most common use of salt is to add flavour. We, as Christians, are in the world to permeate it as salt permeates food. We must enrich it by all the different gifts and qualities we each can bring.

Each gift has it's unique contribution in creating the wholeness of the body of Christ. Dance, drama, music and all the arts can add a richness and bring much glory to God. Banners enable people with creative and imaginative gifts to share them for fulfilment and for the joy of others.

I believe in making the most of any opportunity to present Jesus to those who do not know him. As a member of an Anglican church I am aware of the many opportunities the state church has when its facilities are used for marriages, baptisms and funerals. Here is a chance to share Jesus with those who feel uncomfortable and conspicuous in an unfamiliar setting. Often strangers avoid eye contact and concentrate hard on something else. Let us give them something. Just as posters in buses or waiting rooms arrest attention and are sometimes memorized so banners can be easily assimilated. Let us consider those who want to focus on something while in church buildings and give them God's Word. Banners were once described to me as 'posh posters'. They are attractive and colourful and eye-catching. A little memorized scripture is never wasted. 'My Word shall not return to me empty.' That is a promise from God.

Banners will only be used by the Lord if they are of Him in the first place. Like most things they can be misused. Christians can fall into the fashion trap and must beware of thinking that because others use banners they are an essential tool for worship.

If, in your church, there is a group of people who feel

St Luke's, Maidstone.

their gifts could be used in making banners, then the best check is to pray. If this group cannot or will not pray together then they should not go ahead. If they pray and sense that banner-making is not right for them it will no doubt be because the Lord has alternative tasks. If they pray together and find their desire increases and they bubble over with fresh ideas and have a unity between themselves, then they should go ahead.

It may be only one banner that is made by a group and, if this is what the Lord desires, then it is enough. The group will gain much from praying together, developing and deepening friendships and from the mutual support and encouragement that labour for God will bring.

*   *   *

Alison, who spent three years making banners as a full time job for both churches and individuals before taking up a very different post, said in conversation. 'You cannot do Spirit-filled embroidery if you have not been filled with the Holy Spirit. The Holy Spirit is with me all the time. He first came into my life when I asked Jesus in some years ago. Again and again the Holy Spirit has filled my life in a fresh way'.

Alison also talked about standards. She said, 'The Lord wants us to do our best but He is not concerned that our best has not the same level of perfection as some other folks'. Aim for excellence, but it you don't quite reach it be content'.

Alison gives these instructions on the delicate and attractive method she uses of machine embroidery.

'I am with you always' (see photograph opposite).

1. Draw the design full size and then trace on to artists' tracing paper or greaseproof paper.
2. Turn the tracing back-to-front and transfer the design on to the back of the banner using carbon paper. (It will be back to front).
3. Tack a piece of yellow net over the whole of the front of the banner.

4. Set sewing machine to zig-zag (not too wide, except for sewing rays and lettering). The stitch must be close set.
5. Lay a piece of lemon poly-cotton over the front of the banner. Check it covers the area of design it is intended for. Pin or tack in place. Using a good matching sewing thread stitch from the reverse. You will need to widen the stitch for the rays. Trim the excess fabric from between the rays cutting as close to the stitching as you dare.
6. Build up the design as 5 adding the orange, then green, then brown. Use a heavier brown fabric for the border than for the cross and words.
7. Line as for curtains and then make a broad enough hem at top and bottom to take the cane rods.

Focus on People

by a variety of contributors

Do people need to have skills?

No, these can be developed later. It is important that people are first accepted for themselves and their unique way of looking at life. Through prayer and discussion the Holy Spirit will give ability (another word for power) and inspire with ideas and guide each stage. The same Spirit who lived in Him, lives in us.

A 3D portrayal of Christian released from his burden. *New Covenant Church, Dunstable.*

26

Are right attitudes important?

As the ministry of the Word comes through in banners, so too does any wrong spirit in our hearts. Rebellion, independence and pride must be dealt with. There must be a submitting to each other in love 'in honour preferring one another'. We need to walk in the light together as we prepare something that will hang in the sanctuary. There must be a submission to authority for example, checking through with the leaders any ideas we may have. Our spirit will show in the finished work. 'May the beauty of the Lord our God be upon us and bless the work of our hands.' Psalm 90:17.

How can you involve other people?

House-bound people with plenty of spare time may enjoy doing some of the sewing needed to finish a banner. Someone who is not a Christian may enjoy the creativity and friendship of the group.

How can you enable others?

One person writes:

> My major creative role in the life of the group seems to be to provide the administrative framework within which it operates. I seem to be the one who 'nudges' by proposing dates for planning meetings, then workshops so that we meet our deadlines. I sometimes feel I'm the sheepdog of the outfit and God is the shepherd, the others are His beloved flock so that together we work to His will.
>
> My role in the workshop is to enable the others. I will make the tea, cut out letters, pass an opinion etc. The overriding blessing of membership is the fellowship we have as we talk, share and grow in God. We have all benefitted as God has done new things in our lives and through our hands and minds.

A visit to New Life Church, Durrington, Worthing

What do visitors think of banners in the church?

They make a tremendous impact. People say it's a real joy to see them as they come in. We sometimes take them down and leave the building empty for a short while.

When and how do you meet?

As the next festival or occasion approaches we get together. We are basically 3 or 4 people and 4 or 6 others get drawn into different processes. The organisation is fluid.

Do you ask your pastor for direction?

No, not usually. When trying to create it's hard to be told. But we do sometimes show him sketches and ask his advice. We say 'We've got this idea. How do you feel?'

What about symbols and pictures?

I think you can be over-spiritual and have sunsets, crosses and stars in everything. Why not capture what's fun like wind-surfing and say something with it. I have a longing to be bold with bright colours. I have an idea for a banner one half grey and one half in colour.

What about the cost?

We started with making do from scraps and spent hours fiddling things together. Now we have a generous sum each year and can afford to buy materials. I think Christians can be terribly puritanical and afraid to splash out on tassels, fringes and lovely fabrics. As we're doing it for Him it should be the best we can do.

The one that failed

The original vision was clear and hours of work created a colourful attractive banner. However, whereas the fire and dove were obvious symbols of the Holy Spirit, the leaf shapes and waves proved an enigma! (they were meant to represent wind and water – further symbols of the Spirit). Therefore the full meaning was obscured.

Stages in designing

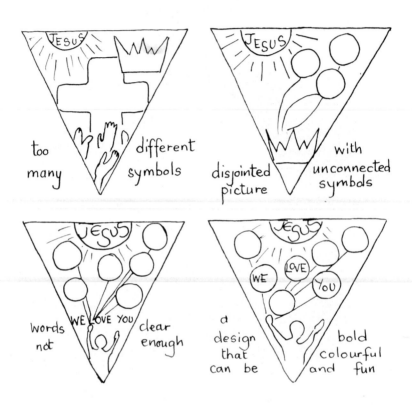

Avoid

- Too many symbols in one banner. The result is confusing. A banner should say one thing.
- Small symbols or designs that give a bitty effect. Instead be bold with your design and blend in the words to give a unified effect.
- Designs that are too abstract or cannot be seen at a distance. Lettering that is too small.

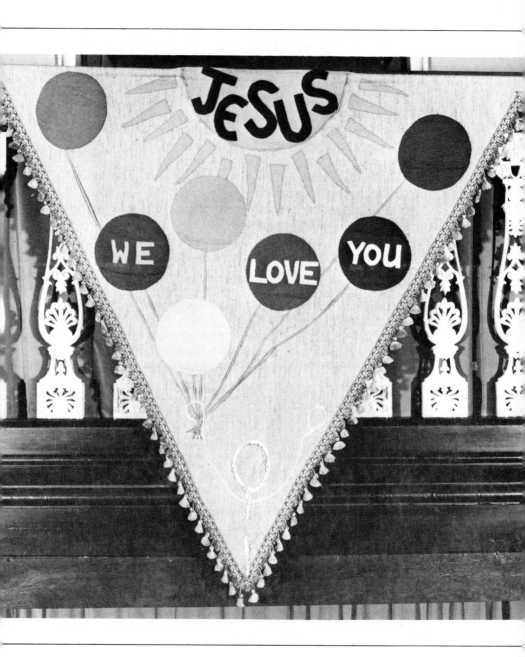

How to achieve 3D effects

1. Pad shapes with cotton wool and wadding.
2. Use cord to give outlines.
3. Use one colour on top of another to give shadow or 3D effect on larger letters.
4. Use several layers of net to give depth.
5. Stitch on shapes ie. the centre of a daffodil that sticks out from the design.
6. Ruckle up material to create a rough surface ie. make a rocky wall around the tomb.
7. Use sequins and beads. These reflect well in artificial light. Large beads can be held in place by a criss-cross of threads.
8. By using different types of fabric.
9. By using several contrasting layers of material to build up a picture.
10. By using wool. This can be couched on to form the bark on a tree trunk or to make the hay in a manger.

'Unless a man is born again he cannot see the Kingdom of God',
John 3:3. The new man rises out of the dark river of his past,
forgiven and filled with the life of Christ.
St Aldate's, Oxford

Batik provides a glowing representation of praising hands and a window and a cross; a focal point in a place of worship.
The King's Church, Amersham

These are clear words to encourage and direct. The high rise blocks and highway are collage and the sky is dyed graduated colours.
The King's Church, Amersham

This small picture could be interpreted in different ways. It was inspired by the Emmaus story. It is framed as a picture for a birthday gift.
Priscilla Nunnerley

Made as a frontal for a youth custody centre chapel, the details of this banner are beautifully embroidered. It has been commented that the polar bear appears to be balancing on a surf board!
The Church of the Holy Spirit, Bedgrove, Aylesbury

The sky effect was achieved by covering up different parts step by step and using car spray paint.
New Life Church, Durrington, Worthing

The rich, vibrant colours are achieved with fabric paint on material. The letters are silver and gold leathercloth and the figure is made of materials.
St Paul's, Howell Hill, Cheam, Surrey

A drawing from the Good News Bible for Psalm 126:5 inspired this picture. The corn sheaves are made from knitting wool couched down and overstitched at the end to form the ears.
The King's Church, Amersham

The background is made with car spray paint and the ears of corn are felt. If words were required there could be a separate banner.
New Life Church, Durrington, Worthing

The words and pictures of Stirling castle and town are a call to the church to be ready and prepared. The contrasts of gold with dark green and black are both clear and dramatic.
Murray Place Baptist Church, Stirling, Scotland

The Risen Reigning Lord. This large banner with its triumphant words was made for Easter. The abstract explosive design emphasises Christ's resurrection.
Murray Place Baptist Church, Stirling, Scotland

The beautiful embroidery indicates the careful tending by the Gardener and the rich fruit produced by the vine.
St Mary's, Maidenhead, Berks

The words are those of Mary from the Magnificat as she exults before the Lord.
Designed and machine-embroidered by Alison Eames for a Blackpool Church

More about the colour photos

Let there be Light

It was all done with car-spray paint. A full-size paper pattern of the banner with the design on was made. The paper was cut to produce stencils for the sun, the clouds and the rays. The pattern was then pieced together again and placed on the white material and pinned. Then each ray was uncovered in turn and sprayed and then recovered, whilst the next one was done. The sun was left white and the clouds were done last and were effective because silver was sprayed round the edges of them, fading into white in the centres.

I am the true Vine. My Father is the Gardener

Some leaves are made of the tie and dye material in shades of green, yellow, white and tan. Others are in plain colours in velvet and a silky material. They are backed with iron-on vilene and are attached to the background with gold chain stitch, which runs down the main veins of the leaves so the edges are free and give a 3D effect. The grapes are circles of taffeta in various colours gathered round the edge and stuffed. They are sewn individually on to a canvas base and attached to the banner.

The people that walked in darkness have seen a great light

Isaiah 9:2

Working with spray paint
by Jill Kingsbury and Vivienne Hayes
(see colour photograph)

The Harvest Field

1. We bought a pale yellow sheet the colour we wanted for the sun.
2. We laid it on the floor and placed a round tin tray face down in position.
3. We had four tins of car *spray paint, red, yellow, orange and blue/grey. We wanted the picture dark at the top, getting paler and then a yellowy creamy band of colour and then darker again. Then it was a case of taking courage and spraying. When spraying on the floor, care has to be taken not to let drips accumulate round the nozzle; we did have quite a few blobs in one spray sky, we made and needed a bird silhouette to disguise a blob!

   The paint has the advantage of stiffening the banner as it dries.

   The exciting bit is taking the tray off again.
4. The corn was done with three shades of hessian, yellow, orange and khaki. A single template was made and traced onto iron-on vilene in biro. We needed twenty corn ears in each colour. Each batch of twenty was ironed on to the hessian, the biro shows through at the back. Several people took some home to cut out and were pleased to have done a small part of the banner.
5. The heads were placed in position and then the stalks were cut out and eventually it was all stuck. Again we had some extra help with this job.
6. The mice were added as a final touch.

* Incidentally spray paint must be used outside or in a well-ventilated room.

New Life Church, Durrington, Worthing.

St Paul's, Howell Hill, Cheam. Made with net, silver leathercloth and red felt on a navy background. A banner for Christmas.

Dye and Batik

by Jane Coulson

(see colour photographs)

Our church, the King's Church, Amersham, is now made up of three congregations and Sue and I felt the leading of the Holy Spirit to make banners for our congregation in the Great Missenden area. We usually meet in a school hall. The banners are for direction, encouragement and as a focal point. The essence of our work is to capture what is in The Lord's heart for His people.

The first banner 'Prepare in the desert a highway for our God' has a red border round it. This helped it to stand out against a muddled background. The sky is dyed graduated by painting blue dye along one half of wet cloth and hanging it upside down to dry. Then yellow dye in the middle of the other side faded out as sunrise. The words coming forward in size are comprised of sun colours, red, orange, yellow and gold. The highway is padded with machine stitching in lines converging on the horizon to give the illusion of a high roadway. This also sets it above the surrounding desert of high rise blocks.

The second banner was 'Behold I make all things new'. The only way I could think of to achieve the very light effect of the fountain was batik; our first attempt. We first chose the cloth, a remnant of creamy textured synthetic fabric similar to dupion. We then applied hot wax from a saucepan. (Use a sugar thermometer if you have one. The wax should be $120° - 140°$C). You can buy batik wax or have a third beeswax to two-thirds paraffin wax but it will also work with all paraffin wax. The wax could be applied with a tjanting spoon or you may find a paintbrush just as good. Both beeswax and the tjanting spoon can be obtained from a good craft shop or from Dryads.

When all the design was waxed on, the cloth was dipped into a bath of cold blue dye and then hung outside, upside

36

Behold,
I make all things
new

down. More dye was then frequently brushed on with a large decorating brush on the bottom half (top when right way round). There was eventually more colour round the sides and top of the design to create the illusion of light in the centre. When dry the fabric was ironed between sheets of white paper inside newspaper to remove the wax. We used white kitchen paper because newsprint does rub off a little. The lettering was outlined with blue and green felt pen for emphasis. Finally we applied silver lamé, silver thread, crystal drops from an old necklace and some sequins for the water, navy-blue fabric rocks and embroidered moss.

The third banner 'Worship the Lord in the beauty of Holiness' is also batik. We took the design from one of our church windows reminding us of the chapel that we belong to in Amersham. The design was drawn on in pencil and waxed; then the cloth was dipped in yellow dye and hung up. Tangerine dye was then splashed on with a paintbrush, sweeping out from the centre of the cross and over the outstretched hands at the bottom of the picture. When this was damp-dry we turned the cloth upside down and painted on the green and blue round the top in a rainbow shape. When the cloth was dry the felt letters were applied, green, turquoise and blue; then gold thread was embroidered along the rays of light coming from the centre of the cross. Next the bright blue satin border, stiffened with iron-on vilene was sewn on with gold russian piping between it and the main picture and finally the banner was given a backing of white sheeting. We used white colour lining for both batik designs because should the light shine through a lovely translucent effect is given. (Also sheeting is large).

Batik is not difficult – just remember to get the wax hot enough so that it permeates the cloth. It is not particularly messy either. You can do it any time of year if you have somewhere to hang wet dyed cloth.

John 12:32 'But I, when I am lifted up from the earth, will draw all men to myself'.
Figures and the cross. *Christchurch, Stone, Staffs.*

Torn paper collage

by Doug and Hazel Rixon

(with Wycliffe Bible translators in Indonesia)

What is torn paper collage? It is taking small pieces of paper of different colours, and using glue to make a picture, design or decoration. Torn paper collages can be small, say A4 size, or smaller or very large, depending on the desire, experience, patience or number of those working on them.

When you try a torn paper collage, start with A4 size of paper. Think of a design or picture and sketch it first. Always sketch it straight onto the paper or card background. A really large collage may be best tackled by a group or a family. Some people may like working with torn paper collage but can't sketch. If so someone who can sketch or illustrate well can put the idea on the paper or card for the others to do. In the sketching of the design it is necessary to show borders of one area or object against another, e.g. land and sky, or sea and sky, because clear definition is important.

Now a word about paper. Good clear colours are needed, and paper that will tear easily: for such paper collect magazines and colour supplements. Squares of coloured paper, tissue paper and some wallpaper can be used. When you see good colours tear them out and keep them in a large envelope or plastic bag. For glue use Polycell or another wallpaper glue, Elmer's school glue or another PVA type glue or Gloy. Copydex is not recommended for this purpose. When completed, clear varnish helps to give a better finish. PVA glue or Elmer's school glue also acts as a varnish and leaves a certain shine.

Choose colours and tear into pieces about the size (not shape) of your thumb-nail. Some paper tears more easily in one direction. Children are inclined to tear either too large

Torn paper collage. *Doug and Hazel Rixon.*

I will extol you my God and my King

or too small. Next put glue around the inner edge of an area or object if large enough, and put the small torn pieces of paper onto the glued surface, going round the edge first, glueing pieces down if necessary. This will give clear definition of areas or objects. Then fill in from the edge until the whole shape or area is covered. Nothing of the background should show through.

When all the paper is on and the glueing is finished and beginning to dry, go round the different objects, letters etc. in black, either with a thick felt pen, or with a brush using black powder paint, mixed thickly. You may need to do this before glueing on any words to be used.

For letters there are three suggestions. You can cut out the letters according to the size, style and colour desired. Secondly they can be collaged with torn paper. This method is easier if the letters are fairly large. Thirdly, letters or even words can be cut from magazines or newspapers etc., or maybe even Letraset and then stuck on. This may mean a lot of searching to find out what is required. If this method is used or the first one, it is better to stick the letters on top of collaged colour, not to leave a space for them to fit in, as it were. It is better to put the glue on the background and not on the letters. It is obviously necessary to get a contrast of colour between background and letters so that the words stand out.

It is better to work with a proper art brush (not too thick). When making shapes for a collage picture, e.g. candlesticks and candles, shapes or people, small flower petals, it is sometimes a good idea not to collage these but to fold the paper and cut symmetrically, then stick over a collaged background. When you have finished the collage, check, using the glue brush, that all the small pieces of paper are stuck down.

All of us have creativity within us that can be used to demonstrate our relationship with the Lord. Torn paper collage is one medium of creativity that we can take, and direct to our Saviour and our God, the Creator of all things.

Paper Banners — St Johns Church Walmley
Sutton Coldfield

allow 300mm extra top and bottom for neatening & hanging

wide selotape on reverse side to reduce danger of tearing and prevent curling of long edges

lettering — cut out of coloured paper and stuck with 'Pritt' or 'Uhu gluepen' (ideally spray adhesive but this is expensive)

background — painted if necessary with ordinary emulsion paint (we usually use white emulsion & added poster paint to give pale colours.)

figures etc — cut out of coloured paper and stuck on as above and then outlined in thick black felt tip pen to give greater definition when viewed from a distance.

1800 mm or any length to suit Location

600 mm

standard width of lining paper from any wall-paper shop.

base — weighted with cardboard.

43

Children make banners

by Lindy Bairstow

Our group at St Paul's, Howell Hill, Cheam in the summer holidays included about thirty children aged 3 – 13. We produced the 'footsteps' banner in a frenzied 45 minutes! The background was already sprayed on but the children could choose where to stick the verse and the colour material for their footprints. The banner has produced more comment than almost any other hung in the church. The children were thrilled that their contribution to the worship was valued equally with the adult banners. Our church encourages family worship and displaying children's work is important to emphasise their involvement.

We had groups of 10 boys and girls for 45 minutes and had to produce a 'quick' banner for use in the service the following day. Car spray paint proved very popular with the older boys! Letters for a verse were cut out and stuck on a blank white sheet, sprayed over and then peeled off to reveal the writing in white. We also used self-adhesive felt, expensive but easy to use and giving super results.

A few thoughts arising from these two experiences

1. Completely finish the blank banner before the session. Children want to see their efforts hung up at once. Plain sheeting and cheap hessian sacking are both effective.
2. If there is only one session the theme, verse and general pictorial aspect must be thought out beforehand. If more time is available the idea can be just a framework in which the children can do 'their own thing', producing spontanaeity and freshness. Ideally the theme should come from the children but this requires even more sessions.
3. Make sure you have plenty of tasks for all who come.

4. I recommend a complete alphabet of card letters, which can be reversed and drawn round on the back of the felt. The older ones can then cut out and stick on.
5. Simplicity is the key to success.

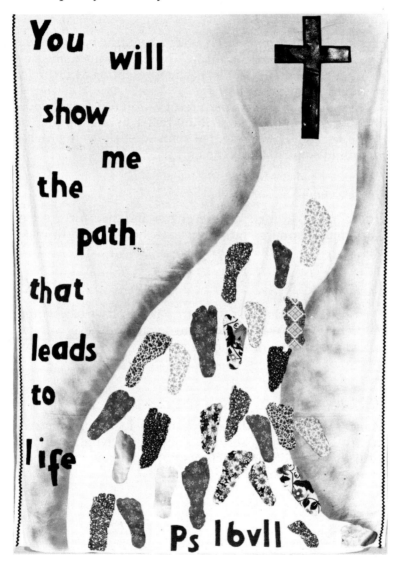

Church involvement

The whole church

Havant Community Church made a beautiful banner of the Good Shepherd and His sheep. The sheep were made by a number of different people, each representing a person for whom they were praying.

They made a similar picture of a Galilean fishing boat and net. Many people contributed a fish to be appliquéd on in the net, which represented someone they were praying for would come to know the Lord.

Housegroups

One church decided on the shape and size for a set of Christmas banners and asked each housegroup to make one.

Teenagers

Ten boys and girls were asked to make a collage of a symbol or picture that was meaningful to them. These were all joined together to form one big picture with words supplied by two of the boys.

10-12 year olds

Made some card and paper banners to be used once a month in the family service. They were given some help with the symbols and pictures but otherwise made them themselves.

St Luke's, Maidstone. The red letters, graduated in size and colour form a beckoning path to the cross.

Banner workshops

This one took place on a Saturday with participants bringing their lunch and hot drinks provided.

A day workshop

10 am. Talk on banner-making with many examples.
11 am. Coffee followed by open prayer. The theme was announced – 'The words of Jesus about nature'. Ten suggestions had been prepared on slips of paper – e.g. vine, water, wild flowers, corn. Each had one or two Bible references. Folk divided into five groups with four in each and chose a subject. So each group did something different. Then they sat round a table meditating on the Bible verses, discussing and drawing ideas. Before lunch some people had chosen background fabrics and started cutting out shapes. An industrious happy afternoon concluded at 3.30 pm. Because of further stitching etc. that needed to be done a date was set three weeks ahead when the banners would be hung in church.

Afternoon workshop

At another workshop the target was completed in three hours on a Sunday afternoon when the theme was 'The Names of Jesus'. Two banners were made with fabric, glue and a little stitching and were hung for the evening service.

Materials used at day workshop

Folk participating brought their own Bibles, paper, pencils, rubbers, sewing kit and scissors. The leader provided visual aids for theme i.e. grapes and an ear of corn, a variety of Bibles including Good News with the pictures, some clear glues, box of cottons and threads, old necklaces, assorted beads, coloured and gold cords, fabric for backgrounds, pieces of felt and scraps of gold and silver plastic kid, cottonwool for padding, sequin waste, odd pieces of wool ideal for tree trunks, net and tulle (white most useful) scraps of odd fabric, leather, fur carpet, iron and board, sewing machine.

A banner day

We gave this name to a gathering of people from different churches who met together in our chapel for a Saturday. Most had already made banners and brought some along. There were so many hanging from every possible nail and rail that we were almost submerged! We started with praise and a talk on the Name of Jesus. Then eight people shared their work and experiences. Some had been asked to talk about specific topics such as machine embroidery, batik, and craft materials and others spoke more generally. The day finished with a lively discussion during which we talked about lettering, symbols and the importance of looking outward and using banners more widely in spreading the good news. The report forms the basis of this book. It was exciting to see what others were doing and the event provided support and stimulation and brought a wider perspective. We do not at the moment have any plans for another day. Why not plan a similar event in your area?

A craft fair

This was a splendid opportunity to display banners for many people to see. The structure of the stall was four wooden posts sunk in the ground in a row with banners hung from cord at three levels. We gave away a photocopied leaflet with several pictures. We combined with another church to run the stall and sat at two trestle tables sewing so that people would see the work in progress and feel relaxed and free to look around.

Colour, backgrounds and fabrics

It was a magic moment in the dim interior of an old French abbey. Suddenly I saw brilliant circles of colour, blue and green, red, orange and yellow dancing on the old grey stone floor. The slate grey background was a superb foil to the brilliance of colour that was summer sunshine coming through a high stained glass window.

The background colour is important. It serves as the right contrast to show up the designs and letters to the best advantage. With light designs a dark or rich colour may be best, with bold or darker designs a light background would be most suitable. If you already have some fabric, stand at a distance from it and judge which colour, designs and letters would be best.

Do not be afraid to be bold. Too many designs are not seen clearly because the background is a nondescript colour that provides no contrast. Consider choosing a colour that will fit in with the meaning. For example, gold is the colour of resurrection and the heavens and green is an everyday colour that communicates growth and rest.

If you are not limited to a colour to express a special meaning then consider more unusual colours like wine, apricot, rust and clover. Sometimes a piece of fabric will inspire an idea, e.g. sea green a fishing design and deep blue a night sky.

Use textured, not patterned fabric for the background. One person prefers needlecord as this gives a fairly stiff finish. Another chooses softer man-made fabric that does not crease e.g. some dress materials. Hessian gives a rough homely appearance and velvet is a rich background for a crown or for flowers. Old curtains or sheets are excellent for large banners. The most economic buy is remnants of cur-

3D effects achieved with carefully cut different shades of felt.
St Giles, Stoke Poges.

51

tain material. We keep two or three basic colours on hand so that if a banner is required it can be started straight away. Our church allocates a generous amount for the group to use during the year. We feel this is important for much time can be wasted searching through bits and pieces which prove inappropriate. We feel the Lord is worthy of the very best.

Most of our banners are based on curtain fabric and many have felt appliqué so they are not washable. They are for now and we do not feel the need to preserve them for posterity. However, they will probably last a long while. Scotchguard spray can be used that protects the fabric.

A good way to line a banner (if it needs it) is to machine the sides like a curtain lining and then turn the top and bottom over and machine or hem in place. A very large banner is best laid face down on the floor with the lining placed on top. Then the edges of the lining should be turned under and stitched in place by hand.

Lettering using iron-on vilene

a) Trace letters with a fine felt tip pen on to the sticky (shiny) side of the iron-on vilene – as close together as possible.
b) Press the materials chosen for the letters and then iron on the vilene in one piece on to the wrong side of the material.
c) Cut out the letters. The vilene backing makes the letters easier to handle, helps prevent fraying and if the glue is applied thinly and evenly, it doesn't seep through the material so much.

Lettering

by various contributors

Simplicity. It is important that lettering on banners does not get too complicated. Calligraphy is observed close but banner lettering must be seen from a distance.

Freehand. Some people have the ability to see the letters in their mind and then put them down on paper.

Books. The Letraset manual is full of ideas. There are many books available. It is good to look at several.

Scissors as a Tool. When cutting round pen marks on fabric, skill can guide the scissors to more detail and more expressive lettering than the pen could achieve.

Enlarge. lettering on a photocopier.

Delicate Lettering. Make templates for letters and draw round these back to front on self-adhesive labels. Then stick these to the felt and cut both out together. Then glue or stitch these onto the background.

Straight Lettering can be obtained by measuring down the side of the banner, pinning at intervals and running cotton across to act as a guide.

Sellotape. It is better to use sellotape rather than pins in sticking paper letters to felt. They will cut out more accurately.

Cord. Use cord to make flowing lettering. Draw first on the background fabric and oversew the cord on.

Embroider round letters or in their centre with chain stitch. Alternatively attach letters with small buttonhole stitch around the edges and embroider with fly-stitch in the centres. With larger letters use cord around the edge to make them more bold.

Wonder Web. Which is adhesive both sides, can be used to attach letters.

Display Ideas

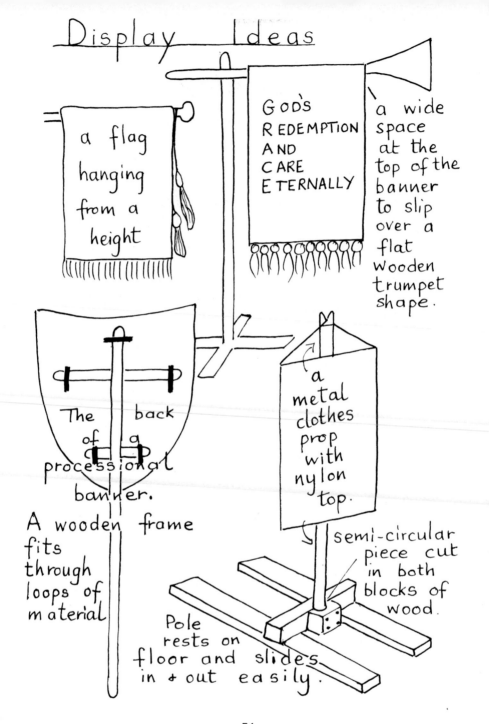

a flag hanging from a height

GOD'S
REDEMPTION
AND
CARE
ETERNALLY

a wide space at the top of the banner to slip over a flat wooden trumpet shape.

The back of a processional banner.

A wooden frame fits through loops of material

a metal clothes prop with nylon top.

semi-circular piece cut in both blocks of wood.

Pole rests on floor and slides in & out easily.

Assorted tips

by various contributors

Transferral of designs

Gill Douglas suggests the following method. 'Having drawn up your design, trace it onto an overhead projector acetate. Pin a large sheet of paper up on the wall (the reverse of odd rolls of wallpaper will do). Project your image on to the paper and draw round it. You then have a complete paper pattern. Transfer the pattern to the background fabric drawing with tailor's chalk or by using a dressmaker's tracing wheel and carbon paper.'

Joining fabric

When sewing together pieces for a large banner join with horizontal seams to eliminate sagging.

Pictures

Brenda Gibbons feels that pictures should speak for themselves and that the design can often stand alone. 'It can express different things to different people and speak powerfully without the need for words. Words can limit a picture to a single meaning when wider interpretation may be more varied and meaningful'.

Sewing draped fabric

Brenda attaches the fabric of the body of the figures with pins and works on the table or floor. Then she hangs the banner on a wall for a few days to observe and also to pin the cloth as it drapes naturally in folds. Then she and her friends sew without using any glue.

A dressmaker's cutting-out board

The squared surface is very useful for enlarging or positioning the design.

Large banners

1. Pin banner under construction to a big *block* board.
2. Use an old-fashioned bed as a frame!
3. Use curtain-lining, weighted tape or broomhandle as a weight.

Pairs

When making pairs of banners you can contrast God's action and our response 'All things come from You' – 'of Your own do we give You'.

Words

Sometimes it is good that the words say something different that adds to rather than repeats what the picture is saying.

Machine appliqué

Gwenda Young suggests the following stages:
1. Tack all pieces into place, pad if necessary for raised effect.
2. Hang in position to see effect and correct if necessary.
3. Machine zig-zag stitching using different coloured thread.
4. Work upwards always to avoid puckering.
5. Work from first layers and untack when picture is complete.

Fringe

Pull crosswise threads out to form a fringe at the bottom.

St Luke's, Watford.

Iron-on Vilene

This can be used to strengthen the background fabric or to make delicate pieces of fabric stiff enough for appliqué.

Circular banners

These can be made by stretching fabric over hardboard which has been cut at the shop. Stitch fabric together across the back.

Outdoor banners

Made of cotton and felt can be sprayed with fabric waterproofing (used for tents and raincoats).

Glues

Uhu, Bondcrete and other clear glues are best to glue material.

Flowers

Those who arrange flowers and those who make banners work in harmony.

WAKE UP!

... to the need
to pray

Posters for a visual age

by Yvonne Coppock

The potential of Christian posters as a tool for evangelism, teaching, challenge and encouragement has been largely ignored. Too often the notice board outside the church remains empty or contains dull notices. We live in a visual age and many people do not have the patience to read books or listen to sermons. One way their attention can be caught is by means of a poster whose message can be assimilated in a few seconds.

Christian posters can perform a similar function to the parables of Jesus. Jesus used word-pictures of familiar situations, often with an unusual element to shock or surprise. He knew these vivid stories would stay in his hearers' minds long enough for them to fathom out their implications. He did not always explain, allowing people the satisfaction of working the meaning out for themselves. Posters are ideal vehicles for this indirect evangelism; they aim to arouse curiosity, sowing the seed of an idea which the Holy Spirit can later cause to germinate and grow. A work of art can touch the emotions and loosen inhibitions, allowing access for the Holy Spirit to work at a deeper level than the rational mind.

At St Paul's Church, St Helier in Jersey, we are blessed with a large notice-board passed each day by hundreds of shoppers, office workers and tourists. For several years a group of us has met for poster workshops. We start with discussion and open prayer, during which the ideas start to flow. We usually work individually on a poster, though there are occasional shared projects. Working side by side we gradually learn to trust each other, exchanging ideas and accepting advice. We change the poster on the notice-board once a week, praying that God will use them to speak to

Poster, *St Paul's, St Helier, Jersey.*

people. If you feel inspired to make posters for your church pray that God will lead you to others with whom you can work. Encourage any who seem interested and discuss the project with your minister.

Experiment with unusual collage materials or unexpected combinations of different media. Try mosaics using small squares of paper or fabric, or a raised design of cut-out polystyrene shapes. Try misty effects with a can of spray paint or coloured cellophane to represent stained glass windows. See what stunning effects you can get with fluourescent paper or starkly simple black and white.

The message to use on your poster may come easily or it may be a struggle to find the right words. As you read the Bible write down verses which suggest a visual interpretation. Make a scrap-book of interesting advertisements, logos and lettering from magazines. Always jot down your ideas as they come. Two golden rules: first, always give a positive message rather than a negative one and second, avoid trying to be too clever. Keep to one idea and keep it simple.

The lettering is important and worth working at as poor lettering will spoil the most interesting design.

With more formal lettering, regularity and good spacing are essential and legibility must be a priority. Make sure the lettering shows up clearly against the background and use as few words as possible.

As well as various fibre tip pens experiment with straight-edged calligraphy pens, drawing pens (such as the Rotring Isograph) and sign-writers' brushes with designers gouache paint. Letraset and stencils give a neat professional effect. Try out your ideas before you start on a poster, planning in pencil and using a ruler where necessary.

Make use of any books you can find on lettering and design. Know the basic rules of lettering before you break them! A Letraset or Chartpak catalogue is a great asset but the book I recommend first is 'Design and Print Your Own Posters' by J. I. Biegeleisen, published by Watson-Guptill Publications, New York. A smaller book with useful hints is 'Posters' by Howard Boughner, published by Grosset and Dunlop, New York. For exciting design ideas try the 'Graphic Design Notebook' by Jan V. White, published by Pitman Publishing Ltd.

One final point. Effective posters may be controversial. If we are going to bring Christ into the market-place we need to use the language people understand and shock tactics may be needed to attract their attention. Soak the whole project in prayer, be willing to put aside your own poster if necessary and be lovingly sensitive to the feeling of other church members. God does not want great artists for this ministry but those who are willing to submit their talent to his authority. Our pride can be the biggest hindrance to his glory. May God richly bless you in your poster-making!

If you have any experience of making Christian posters please write and let us know. We are investigating the possibility of a book and would like to hear how other churches have tackled the subject. Please write to either Yvonne Coppock at 7 Belvedere Drive, St Saviour, Jersey, Channel Islands or to the Editor at her home address on the outside of the back cover.

Visual ideas and resources

Photoposter. Enlarge a colour print to poster size and have it framed behind glass. A photoposter of a field of sunflowers has hung for a year in our church lounge and is now replaced by a photo of a waterfall in a wood in springtime. Letraset words can be put on if desired.

Mobiles. Five angels were suspended by fishing line in space! (for Christmas). Butterflies, doves and fish are all quite easily made from card.

Hardboard banners giving a very stiff and flat finish were made to go on the pillars of Christchurch, Stone, for a Remembrance Day service that was being televised. Pieces of wood that had been curved on one side were glued to the back of the hardboard so it could fit on the pillars.

Small flags were used to wave in praise and worship.

Tablecloth, this could have designs in two corners or sides and could be particularly useful and attractive for meetings in a rented building.

Books relevant to banner-making

The two most helpful books on the subject that were printed in America are unfortunately out of print.

However, *The Folk Arts in Renewal* by Patricia Beall and Martha Keys Barker, Hodder & Stoughton £2.95 and *Worship* by Graham Kendrick, Kingsway £1.95; are relevant reading although they only have a little about banners.

Appliqué by Evangeline Shears and Diantha Fielding, Pan £2.95 is an excellent paperback.

Design in Embroidery by Kathleen Whyte, Batsford £12.95 is a comprehensive book.

Many excellent appliqué and embroidery books are available.

Tiberias Crafts

John and Jean Wright run a well-stocked craft shop and welcome telephone enquiries for more details. A mail-order catalogue with church banner-makers in mind is available for two first-class stamps. 61 The Street, Ashtead, Surrey. Tel. Ashtead 77727.

They sell specialist items such as gold and silver leather-cloth by the inch or yard, gold bouillon, gold and silver lace and braids.

Felt, all colours 12 inch square is available in red/blue/green/black, 18 inch wide self-adhesive felt by the yard, especially good for lettering and children's work.

Flower petals and stamens.

Gold and silver sprays for backgrounds, stencils and highlights (use car spray for large areas of other colours!).

Sequin waste, red, silver, gold and pearl white, cheap and good for children to use.

Fabric paints from the Deka range, 'Deka Silk' for fine cotton, silk, polyester – a water-colour effect best used on a white background and can be sprayed using a diffuser. 'Deka Permanent' for heavier weight materials – paint on direct or stencil or print, with leaves, potatoes, plasticine or biscuits!

Fabric crayons for children. Crayon on to paper and iron on to fabric (remember it comes out in reverse).

Fabric markers (quilting pens) for drawing on to material – vanishes when slightly wetted.

Embroidery transfer pencils – trace a pattern from anything, then turn over and iron on.

Outreach possibilities

1. Take a banner workshop.
2. Write in someone else's parish magazine.
3. Write in a local newspaper.
4. Have a banner library. Lend to others.
5. Exhibition in local library. Craft exhibitions. Exhibition in holiday areas. Large halls/exhibition areas.
6. Use in big meetings/crusades. March of witness. Banner across street. Carnivals. Street drama. Over hospital bed. House of bereaved. Weddings and funerals.
7. Send to missionaries – for their home and use in evangelism (words in the correct language).
8. Give them away.

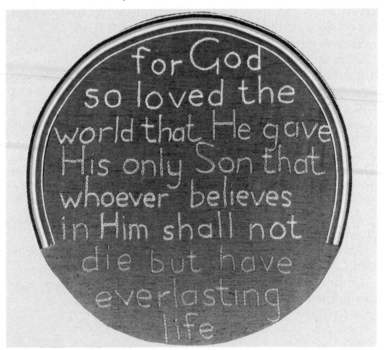

This was made for a doctor's surgery.